MW01657125

WE STOOD THE LINE

Alan D. Soderfelt

This book is dedicated to
Jesus: for letting me make it back from Vietnam,
Cpl. Felidelphio B. Gomez: my best friend, and
Heidi Soderfelt Omerza: who thanked me for being a Vietnam veteran before it became a popular thing to do.

WE STOOD THE LINE

This book is for all the Marines who stood the line in Vietnam but came back without a Purple Heart or any other medal of honor. They went on all their patrols and their share of ambushes and listening posts. They were over there for twelve months, and they did it all.

Don't get me wrong, I respect and appreciate the Marines who were wounded and sent home in a month or two. But then there are the other guys: the ones who served their entire tours of duty in Vietnam, yet don't get the respect they deserve just because they didn't receive any medals of honor. Those men dodged bullets, carried out the wounded, were thirsty and tired, and usually too hot, as well. They are the unsung heroes we don't talk about or give credit to... but they served in Vietnam for twelve @#$%& months!!

PREFACE

This book is a collection of stories about my two tours of duty as a Marine in Vietnam. I wrote it to enlighten some family members who think I had it a lot worse over there than I really did. Friends and relatives of Marines who served during that time would enjoy this book, too

It took many years for me to get started on this book (life got in the way). Once I decided on which stories to share, I created the rough draft using speech-to-text software. And then one of my daughters helped me with the editing and formatting.

I served in the Marine Corps infantry for two tours of duty from March 1965 to December 1966 (I only know those dates because I looked them up). The first tour was for eleven months, and the second was for six.

The stories I tell are true. I remember some as though they happened yesterday; there are others that

I've had to think about for a while. I don't always recall which tour events took place in.

I was on the following large operations: STARLITE, PIRANHA, HARVEST MOON, BLUE MARLIN #1, and BLUE MARLIN #2. And heaven knows how many smaller operations I was on.

I didn't write about my time in boot camp; that has already been covered quite well in movies and books. I also didn't write about the history of the Vietnam War.

I'd like to say to the younger generation that serving in Vietnam was really, really rough. I don't know if you can put yourself in that frame of mind since there are so many video games out there where you run and shoot and kill the enemy without even breaking a sweat. It wasn't that way at all. And it wasn't all killing and blood and guts, either. But it was so hot, and we were really thirsty, and damn, we were tired.

In combat, you weren't given time to grieve when you lost a close friend. You grieved in silence, with no time alone or with other people who loved him.

There was no grief counseling; instead, you had to saddle up and move out, hiding the tears in your eyes. No matter what happened or how you felt, you kept right on going. At night, you felt even worse, but you knew you'd make it through somehow because the Marines before you had made it through situations that were similar.

In Vietnam, we Marines were so close to each other that we didn't put much faith in anything else. What kept us going was each other, not Mom's apple pie, the girl next door, or anything like that. Every Marine believed that any other Marine would take a bullet for him and vice versa. In order to get back home, we knew we could only count on each other.

Alan D. Soderfelt
WeStoodTheLine@gmail.com
December 2021

FIRST DAY IN VIETNAM

My first day in Vietnam was unforgettable; I still recall every detail. Young and bright-eyed, we'd finished our guerrilla training in Okinawa and were finally going to put it to use.

They planned for us to go ashore that day. When they told us to go get our ammunition, grenades, and signal flares from our compartments, we knew our training was over, and we were really going to hit the beach just like they did in World War II.

Over the PA System, we were ordered to go to our depart stations. On our way to our assigned areas, we noticed little Mike boats bobbing up and down in the water.

A troop carrier ship--like the ones in World War II--transported us that day. And, just like in the movies, little Mike boats were standing by to take us to shore.

When they threw the rope nets over the ship's side, we knew the time had come for us to prove ourselves as fighting Marines. The sea was calm, so climbing down the rope nets shouldn't have been difficult, but the weight of our packs made it hard.

Once a Mike boat was loaded, it would pull away from the ship and make circles in the water. Then, on a certain sign, they all lined up and headed for the beach.

Over the walls of the Mike boat, we could see bombs exploding and jets dropping napalm--it was quite a sight! (Later, we learned that everything had appeared closer than it really was.)

As our little boat headed for the beach, we were all concerned about what day's end would bring. We'd trained hard, and we were good, but the enemy soldiers fought hard and were good, too.

They said for us to run toward the beach at the drop of the gate. The gate dropped. We ran so fast... but soon we noticed that nobody was shooting at us, and all we saw were little girls selling bottles of Coke.

THE ENEMY

I went to Vietnam with the idea that we'd be fighting enemy soldiers who only had outdated weapons like spears. I thought our biggest concerns would be stakes swinging from trees or getting caught in some kind of old trap. We were young and brave and had attitudes of "bring it on!"

But it turned out that our enemy had weapons that were just as good as ours and knew how to use them, too.

People used to say that the night belonged to the Vietnamese, but we were just as good, if not better, than they were at day or night fighting.

One advantage the enemy soldiers did have was they got more sleep than we did. We went on patrol or had all-night ambushes on many nights, then would have to be on patrol or stand watch again the next night.

We were so exhausted and sleep deprived that they could choose their time and place for us. Sometimes, they would succeed. Most of the time, however, we would throw a few grenades and fire our weapons at them, and they'd be gone until next time.

There's no way of knowing how many times they attempted to attack us but didn't do any damage. People consider them great fighters because they only remember the few times they succeeded.

They probably had more patience than us, but that was about it. As Marines, we usually wanted to get it done now; it took us a long time to learn how to be more patient with our movements and on ambushes.

MEDEVACS

After breakfast at base camp, we found out that we'd be taking helicopters to our patrol area that day. All in all, we thought it would be a good day because we'd get to ride there in helicopters and a couple of dogs were coming with us to search out caves.

After everyone deboarded, we started down a small trail that we were okay with taking. *The dogs will protect us from the booby traps.* Even though the dogs got riled up a few times, all they found were some holes. We all made it through that morning no worse for the wear.

By the time afternoon rolled around, the suffocating heat and humidity were getting to us, so we took a break. Word was passed that we'd stopped just so the dogs could cool down... but they weren't cooling down. They tried everything to help those overheated dogs, but nothing worked.

They gave up and called a medevac for the dogs, but our radioman was told that there weren't any codes in the codebook about medevac'ing dogs. After confirming that yes, it was the new codebook we were using, our radioman was again asked to repeat what he wanted. He then stated quite clearly that we have dogs suffering from heat exhaustion that must be medevac'd now or else they will die. A few seconds of silence passed before the voice on the radio said he didn't understand.

The company commander got on the radio and, with a few choice words, made it clear that the dogs had to be medevac'd out of there immediately. After a long pause, he was finally told that a medevac was on its way.

Later, while the dogs rode home in a medevac, we humans had to hurry up in the heat to make up for lost time! We joked for the next few weeks about how a bunch of raggedy-ass Marines loaded down with full gear could out-hump military dogs carrying nothing.

DANGER DIDN'T MAKE ME FEEL MORE ALIVE

I believe it's true when people say that much of war is routine. Reinforcing your fighting hole, getting water, getting resupply, and eating were routine to us. Even things like going on patrols or setting up and waiting for ambushes were routine most of the time.

The times you were under attack or attacking were terrifying. Some will say that was when they felt the most alive; I never felt that way or got to that point. I only felt scared and wished it was over with and that I'd never have to feel that way again.

When you were at base camp or a good perimeter, you had your everyday fear, which wasn't too bad. It's hard to explain, but you always felt safer in your own area even though the VC were all around you. And the better you knew a place, the safer you felt.

On a large-company patrol, you weren't very afraid since there were so many other Marines around. It was about the same when you were on a small patrol during daylight hours because you had already worked with everyone before.

One of the most fear-inducing situations was being on a night ambush and hearing sounds that sounded like they'd come from something larger than the small animals we heard sometimes. Your heart pounded as you strained your eyes to see what was coming for you in the darkness. You waited for what seemed like forever--but was only a few minutes--only to find out that those scary sounds were actually just a couple of wayward civilians. It always took a while to calm down again.

The fear was off the charts when you were ambushed, under mortar attack, or flying into a very-hot landing zone. And no, I didn't feel more alive than ever at those times--I only felt fear and lots of it.

I'm happy to say that I wasn't deathly afraid very often, but I didn't want to ever feel that way again when I did. The everyday fear--just walking patrols or standing guard duty at night--was quite enough for me.

When I got back to the States, it was hard to believe how much danger and stress I'd been through. I often wonder how anyone ever made it through a whole tour of duty without getting shot or losing his mind.

WATER

The United States Marine Corps tried to give the troops what they needed out in the field. Water was one of those needs. And finding water to drink was always a primary concern of ours.

On a small hill overlooking a creek, we ended up needing water more than ever before. (We couldn't drink the water from the creek below: it was barely flowing and had bodies in it.) With rolling hills and dark-green grass in the distance, it was quite picturesque.

But the top of the hill wasn't so great: the Marines before us hadn't removed the bodies of the enemy soldiers. It was hard to breathe and flies were everywhere. And the situation worsened as the day grew hotter.

After hiking all morning in the jungle, we were thirsty and hot, so we called for a supply of water. We waited and waited for the water. Finally, we heard the familiar sounds of a helicopter. But our relief soon turned to disappointment when we saw what the helicopter brought us: no water and roll after roll of barbed wire! And, by that time, it was too late to call for another helicopter.

Knowing that at first light a helicopter would arrive with water and C-Rations, we somehow made it through the night. And it did arrive at first light with more @#$%& barbed wire!

Having no other choice, our company commander sent a squad with everyone's canteens to get water from the filthy creek below. The corpsman wasn't happy about that because that water wasn't fit to drink, but our purification pills would help with that.

The "purified" water ended up looking, tasting, smelling, and feeling just as disgusting as we'd thought, but nobody got sick. I guess by that time our bodies knew they'd have to take what they got and not complain too much.

DESCRIPTIONS

HUMPING

Humping is walking with a heavy backpack on your back. A backpack so heavy--ours weighed 60 lb or more--that it makes you hunch over. And you are forced to hunch over because you will fall backwards if you attempt to stand up straight.

WEATHER

The heat and humidity took their toll on us. Sweat poured down our faces, got in our eyes, and dripped down our backs.

Then there was the cold: we froze for a few weeks. Not literally froze, but it was impossible to stay warm when the wind was blowing and the rain was pouring down.

You're probably wondering why we didn't have more clothing or blankets to keep us warm. Since we had to carry everything we had day and night, there was no room for anything more; we ended up with just our ponchos.

If you tried to get some sleep after guard duty in cold weather, the hours of shivering and shaking you'd just endured would have exhausted you so much that you'd pass out more than fall asleep.

WATER

The water we drank may have come from a bomb crater, a fast-moving stream, or a stagnant rice paddy. We didn't get much of a choice about what we drank during the hot season--just about any kind of liquid was acceptable to drink at that time.

Water was always a concern except during the rainy season. With the 90-degree temperatures and all the gear we carried, it never lasted as long as we wanted it to. (Although we always had to worry about and search for water, we never ran out of ammunition or C-Rations.)

HOT MEALS

The only hot meals I had there were made out in the field. They were better then C-Rations but not by much. When hot meals for Thanksgiving and Christmas were brought out to our location, we were extra alert because we were sure that Charlie knew what was going on, too. And we ate fast so everyone would get a chance to eat.

The hot meals were good, but they were such a hassle. Due to the hassle, I think most of the men would have rather had a few extra C-Rations and a couple of beers.

SLEEPING

Other than my arrivals to and departures from Vietnam, I never slept in a large building with a roof. I slept in the bush.

HOME

We did have a perimeter sometimes that we called home, and we did keep some of our personal gear there. At one point, we had small tents and cots, but that didn't last very long. One of the places we called home had a small lake we used for swimming and bathing, and another was close to a village that sold ice and sodas.

MORNING ROUTINE

Our established morning routine was followed unless we'd had an eventful night. We returned from night ambush or night watch, cleaned our weapons, ate a breakfast of C-Rations and coffee (only base-camp coffee was hot), and then were given our orders. Our usual orders were to search and destroy the enemy.

RADIO

We didn't like having the radio in our area--its long antenna could be seen by the enemy. And even in noisy environments, we could hear it when the button to talk was pushed. On the other hand, it was nice to have it nearby when we needed to call in artillery or air support.

OPERATIONS

No matter how large the operation was, it usually broke down into squad-size patrols or even fire teams that operated on their own, with the big unit giving the orders where to go and when.

LISTENING POSTS

A listening post--usually made up of 1-3 men--goes out 20 or 30 yards and just listens for the enemy. When they hear something, they alert the Marines on the line as soon as possible.

PATROLS

We'd start out on our patrols in the morning and return before dark. Many things could delay our return to base camp--rugged terrain, hot weather, sniper fire, etc. With such a small group of Marines, we didn't want to risk being out in the bush after dark, so we'd take our chances on a trail to increase our chances of getting back before night. It usually worked out all right, but sometimes we'd pay for being careless.

WILDLIFE

Although jungles are known for exotic animals, I mostly only saw lizards; I guess we were too loud for the exotic animals to come around. I did hear from a friend that some Marines had seen lions and monkeys over there.

And then there were the leeches. Places with a lot of moisture had leeches everywhere; they dropped from the vines and elephant grass, and came right up from the ground. When you went on a patrol in a wet area, you'd end up with leeches all over your body.

I didn't really mind the leeches; I considered them harmless little critters. They would usually drop off and leave you alone once they'd had enough of your blood. They were certainly better than the mosquitoes that were always around, yet some Marines would get panicky just at the sight of leeches.

I recall a patrol where we really, really wanted to take a break right away so we could remove all of the leeches from our bodies. Once we got to a drier area, we used salt and cigarette butts to remove them.

Later that night, wrapped up in my shelter, I felt something on my leg. *It's a leech!* I smashed it a few times, but it wouldn't come off. I tried pulling it off with my fingernails, but it still wouldn't budge.

After covering myself the best I could, I used a flashlight to see what was going on. It turned out that the leech I'd been trying to remove for so long was actually a mole that I'd had all my life! I then forgot all about leeches and fell asleep.

A CLEAR VIEW ALL AROUND

We spent most of our time in lush vegetation, not knowing what was around the corner or even two feet in front of us. Every new location was dangerous in some way, but we got used to living like that.

We all decided that going to the DMZ (Demilitarized Zone) would be good since the vegetation there would be gone either from Agent Orange or bombings, which would give us a clear view all around.

But once again, we hadn't thought things through. If we could see all around us, then the enemy could see us, too. In fact, we felt like fish in an aquarium there, so we had to stay spread out and off the skyline (but it was all skyline to us). When we crossed over hills or even just walked around, it seemed like we were always standing out and making silhouettes of ourselves--something that Marines just don't do.

We also didn't like how there was no water to be found there, so we had to depend on helicopters re-supplying us. We were careful not to drink all of our water until we saw the helicopter land. We were thirstier than usual since there was no shade to protect us from the sun. And you'd think there would've been some wind on that hilltop, but there wasn't.

Although there weren't any leeches or bugs at the DMZ, we still had to deal with mosquitoes. They flew in and out at their leisure.

Despite feeling like we were living in a fish bowl, we didn't have any casualties during our time on that hill. And we did become a little more at ease there after a couple of weeks. (We became a little more comfortable at every new location after a week or two.)

When we relocated to our next location, we were actually glad to be getting back to the jungle we'd dreaded so much before, where we depended on our sense of hearing more than anything (but so did Charlie).

TRAILS

We were warned to stay off trails as much as possible, but when it was in the high 90s and very humid, we didn't want to be whacking our way through jungle bushes, so we split the difference. If the bushes weren't too bad, we went through them. If not, we found a trail to take. (One option increased our risk of getting ambushed, while the other increased our risk of stepping on booby traps.)

We had to be more alert on a trail. Two or three people could walk on a trail with no issues, yet the next one could still get blown off.

It was always something. If we were taking too long to reach our destination--no matter where we were going--we had to pick up the pace. And that meant letting our guard down a bit and taking a path so we could make up time. (Nobody wanted to risk spending the night out in the bush with only a few men.)

NIGHT PATROL IN A NEW LOCATION

We were moving to a different hill, but they wouldn't set us down on that hill, of course. No, they had to put us about 100 meters from it. Why couldn't they just set us down on the hill itself? I had no idea. I never knew what the people at headquarters were thinking.

We got off to a late start that day and made bad time due to the heat and humidity. We arrived at our new location just as it was getting dark, then set up our perimeter and fields of fire the best we could at that time of day. Since we didn't know that area's weak spots, we would have to stay awake and be more alert than usual for a night or two.

Later, the powers-that-be surprised us with orders to go on a patrol that night, which was a bad idea since it was our first time there. Nobody could think of a good reason for a night patrol on that particular night.

I'd learned a lot about the night in Vietnam. When I first arrived, I thought that when the sun went down, the moon came up soon after, but that wasn’t true. If it wasn’t completely dark, we could move well at night: give us a little moonlight and the stars, and we'd be okay. If only the stars were out, then there'd be enough light for us to move around. But an overcast sky would make it too dark to move around easily. There wasn't much light that night, so there must've been mostly just stars.

We begrudgingly began our patrol. (We weren't in good moods since that patrol had messed up our plans to catch up on some much-needed sleep.)

After just a minute, machine-gun and small-arm fire was opened up on us. We lay down quickly and stayed still as bullets flew overhead.

When a friend of mine saw the tracer bullets--bullets that give off some light so you can see where they're headed--flying by, he remarked that he didn't want to get hit by one of those because it would burn more than a regular bullet.

We heard Marines yelling and cursing in the distance about how there'd been some kind of miscommunication that resulted in us getting shot at.

We were wondering why the hell they'd shot at us, and they were wondering why the hell we'd been so off course and close on their side.

We hadn't thought that the listening post would be out so far. And we definitely hadn't thought it would have a machine gun. And why had *they* been out so far? Usually, a listening post is just 20 or 30 yards from the front. If they heard something, then the Marines at the listening post were supposed to get to the front as fast as possible to relay the information so the line could be 100% alert.

Thank God nobody got shot. Tempers were hot, but those would cool down soon enough.

After all that, we still had to go on our patrol. By that time, however, I was certain there were no enemy soldiers in the area. They definitely knew we were there and didn't want anything to do with us. I'm sure they'd gotten up and moved, probably chuckling a little bit, wondering what the hell we were doing out on our first night in a new location.

Later that night, we made it to and from our checkpoints with no additional issues.

I still think about how lucky we were that night and how my friend didn't want to get hit by a tracer bullet. Just another night in Vietnam...

THE DAYS THAT DIDN'T RUN TOGETHER

The days ran together over there. There were no vacation days or weekends off, so it didn't really matter what day it was.

We did know when it was Sunday, but not because a priest or a rabbi would stop by. (I'd heard good things about priests and rabbis over there, and I'm sure they would have if they could have, but they just weren't up to jumping on helicopters to go out in the field only to talk to us when there were thousands of Marines in the staging area.) We always knew when it was Sunday because a corpsman would pass out large anti-malaria pills on Sundays.

I'd heard stories about some men refusing to take the anti-malaria pills, but that didn't happen in our outfit thanks to all the movies and stories that had instilled so much fear in us. And not taking them would have put other Marines in danger (we were already so short-handed that losing just one man to illness would have hurt us).

If you did get malaria, it would only take you out for a little while until your fever would drop enough for you to be considered recovered. No matter how bad you felt, you could be back out in the bush in a week.

We also knew when it was the Marine Corps birthday, Thanksgiving, Christmas, and New Year's because they would go out of their way to serve us a hot meal on those days. However, I believe that most Marines would've preferred some beer and a few C-Rations over a hot meal. One reason was that due to having to schedule the patrols around the hot meal, we always worried that Charlie would know what was going on and be more likely to strike at that time.

I'm not saying the food wasn't good, but it did seem like a lot of trouble for a lot of men, and most of us could've waited until the next year when we'd be able to have a hot meal at home.

MORTAR ATTACK

It was a day like any other day: I always say that, but most of the time it really was. In the rainy season, it would rain like the day before, and in the summer, it would be hot like the day before, so I'm not off by much.

On the day this story took place, we had our usual orders to search and destroy the enemy. The location must have been far away because a helicopter took us there.

We moved along at a good rate for a long time, taking in the wonderful scenery. Suddenly, we heard mortar shells coming our way.

In the Marine Corps, you are taught to go toward your enemy, but when there are mortar shells coming and they're the small ones, you pick up and run in an orderly manner. Running will get you away from the mortar shells because the enemy soldier can't move the mortar stand fast enough to be accurate. You're not outrunning the mortar shells; you're outrunning the man who is trying to kill you with them.

Once we were far enough away to slow down, we called in our artillery. We never knew what happened after that since we didn't go back to check.

That was our excitement for the day. We humped up and down the hills for the rest of it. And, once again, our biggest concern was finding water to drink.

Just another day in Vietnam...

STRESS

It's hard to believe how much pressure a person is under 24 hours a day in battle--but there wasn't a battle every day. Believe it or not, there were even some days that were slow ones.

If you were out on patrol in the same area for quite a while, then you knew the enemy soldiers probably weren't around. If one or two did remain, they would've run away as soon as they saw you. Situations like that didn't worry us much.

You were under a lot of stress when they helicoptered you to a rough area that they'd warned you about in advance. Likewise, making a helicopter landing while the enemy soldiers are already shooting at you before your feet hit the ground... talk about stress!

On a patrol or ambush at night, your heart would pound when lying there waiting for enemy soldiers to come by so you could ambush them. Yet there was always the chance they'd already seen or heard you, and were just waiting for the right time to attack.

The elephant grass unnerved you on patrols because it made it impossible to see anything in front of you. As you pushed it down, you had no idea what was on the other side. It was probably just more grass, but you never knew.

No matter what, you always felt safe at your base camp or anywhere else you'd been set up for a few days. You felt that way because you weren't on the move and other Marines were around to help take care of anything that could happen.

Surprisingly, the situation that gave me the most stress--more than I'd ever had in Vietnam--was sleeping under clean, white sheets at a United States military base. That feeling of safety gave me a chance to think about how much danger I'd been in.

One thing was for sure: no matter how relaxing your day was going, all of that could change in an instant, and then you'd suddenly be getting issued more ammunition and filling up canteens to go somewhere you really didn't want to go. It was a feeling that's hard to explain to somebody who hasn't experienced it.

It’s one thing to be under stress for a few days, but to feel that way for a year or more, knowing that every day could be your last, is stress that just doesn't go away. It was when you got back to the States that you really started thinking about the danger you'd been in over there. And then you thanked God that you'd made it back safely.

UNIFORMS

I can only just imagine how bad we smelled and looked at times in the bush. We looked nothing at all like the Rifle-Squad or Marine-Band Marines you see in pictures wearing Dress Blues.

We all smelled bad, and there wasn't much we could do about it. After a while, you didn't even notice anymore until a new person would tell you how great you smelled.

We had no way to get clean out there in the bush. We would swim and clean ourselves off in a stream, but we rarely came across streams large enough for that. And we knew the enemy soldiers spent their time near water, too. I'm sure they had their eyes on any body of water that was good enough for swimming, so we usually had to skip getting clean (unless friendly forces happened to be nearby).

I vaguely recall taking showers somewhere, but that must have only happened once or twice. I was raggedy and dirty just about every day. One of the places we called home there had a small lake that we went in sometimes.

We must've had enough water for shaving because I've never seen any Marines with facial hair in photographs. Since there were no members of the press taking pictures where we were, we shaved mostly to keep the little critters off.

We wore our uniforms until they literally fell off: our pants disintegrated as we walked. The only time we received new uniforms was when they changed from Marine Corps green to a camouflage pattern.

They must've given us new boots when we needed them since they never wore out, even with all the walking and humping we did. And all the moisture and muck and mud would've made getting new boots a priority. As many miles as I walked and humped, I never had to worry about my boots.

HELICOPTERS

The helicopter is different from an airplane in many ways. An airplane, by design, wants to fly and will do so quite well if there's no interference. A helicopter, on the other hand, does not want to fly. And helicopters do not glide like airplanes do when their engines fail--they just drop.

My first thought prior to boarding a helicopter was always that it wasn't a new one. (Although they were maintained very well, there usually wasn't enough money for new parts.) Then, I'd ask myself why I was going to let it take me to a place where people could and would shoot at me. Of course, I had no choice.

The helicopters were always loaded to their maximum load. We knew that because we'd first load 10 or 11 people on a helicopter, then have one person dismount if it couldn't take off. That's how we knew the helicopter was carrying its maximum load and wasn't going to stay up if anything happened to the engine.

Another thing you learned fast about helicopters was that if a helicopter was going to pick you up, then it would almost always be taking you to a hot spot. When it took you down, every VC around knew your location and was headed your way to harass you. That's why you always jumped off the helicopter as fast as you could. And those jumps weren't easy, either.

Helicopters make good targets, too. One helicopter we were in was shot at a couple of times, but that didn't stop us from jumping off since the damage was minimal.

Once in a while, we got lucky and a helicopter would return us to base camp. That rarely happened; we usually returned by foot, conducting search-and-destroy operations along the way.

Despite my complaints, helicopters weren't as bad as I make them seem. Helicopters took us to hot spots, but they also kept us in ammunition and C-Rations, supplied us with water, and transported our wounded, too.

SOUNDS

There were sounds all around us in the jungle, but some stood out more than others, like those of a rifle being shot, mortar rounds exploding, and artillery shells whizzing by overhead. There were also the sounds of little animals crawling around and snakes looking for food. And the one a radio makes when its button to talk is pushed.

We heard enemy soldiers in the bush moving, groaning, moaning, and speaking from time to time. We got to know all of the sounds and how to react to each one, too.

The sound that worried us the most was no sound at all, especially on a night ambush or a night watch around the perimeter: it meant there were people nearby who wanted to hurt us or kill us.

Sounds still affect me to this day. Silence makes me feel like something bad is about to happen. And I still crouch down when there's a sudden noise. The noises usually last for only a moment, so I can sometimes stop my reaction to them.

The sound that's stayed with Vietnam infantry veterans the most is that of helicopter blades cutting through the air. It will stay with me until the day I die because it usually meant something bad. Thank God the helicopters were there, but it seemed like it was never for a good reason.

They put you on a helicopter when another company or battalion was in trouble or when you had a big operation with a battalion, which meant there would be casualties. Also, helicopters would come in for medevacs. When you were on patrol and there were too many enemy soldiers, support fire from the helicopter would've been called in.

I'm sure if you took a helicopter for a sightseeing tour of the Grand Canyon, then its sound wouldn't bother you. That wasn't the case with Marines in Vietnam, though.

Whenever I heard a helicopter, I don't know if what I felt was fear, but it wasn't a good feeling to have. Even though you would've liked to be

helicoptered out to the bush--much better than walking--you knew there'd always be a price to pay.

DON'T FALL ASLEEP

When it was your turn at watch, you were expected to stay awake no matter how much you'd done that day or the day before. Judging by the number of stories I've heard about Marines falling asleep on watch, however, I'm sure the percentage who did so was quite high.

Despite my firsthand experience with exhaustion and sleep deprivation, I still didn't understand how anyone could've fallen asleep on watch with the enemy always around. My best guess was that he probably made himself as comfortable as possible and then rested his head on a sandbag, or something like that.

Confident that I wouldn't actually fall asleep, I tested my theory the next time I was on watch. The next thing I knew the lieutenant was chewing me out and threatening that he'd have something for me later on.

The lieutenant's plan for me and two other Marines was to put us out on a listening post on our next company-size operation. I guess he figured that if we fell asleep there, the rest of the company would hear the enemy dragging our dead bodies away, and that would be enough of a warning for anyone.

You'd think that three men who were already caught sleeping on watch wouldn't make for a good listening post, but that wasn't true. We definitely didn't fall asleep out there; it was just too damn scary, even with three Marines. We stayed awake. There was no action that night--thank God for that.

The time a lieutenant caught me sleeping on watch ended up being the only time I did so. I never again allowed myself to get comfortable on watch, and I forced myself to sit up straight or stand if I could.

NIGHT WATCH

Like I've said before, we never got enough sleep in Vietnam. And night watch was just one of the many things that robbed us of it. After your watch, you'd find a place to curl up right away to avoid missing a minute of precious sleep. You could always eat or drink at a later time, but not sleep.

Night watches became routine after a while, but there was one night watch so terrifying that I thought my time had come.

At the time of that watch, we didn't have enough men to stay in each fighting hole, so we'd have to walk from place to place all night long. It really didn't make much sense, but that's what we were told to do.

It was one of those dark, dark nights, and the rain made it impossible to see or hear anything. On nights like that, you wouldn't be sticking around to hang out with the guy who relieved you since it was just too damn cold and wet out, and you were so tired, too.

A few hours after midnight, it was finally my turn to take the watch, and that watch just happened to be the one my best friend was on. Immediately upon seeing me, he quickly filled me in on the latest information regarding the watch--which wasn't much because nobody was out on that cold, dark, rainy night except the crazy Marines--and waved goodbye. After taking just a couple steps into that dark night, I couldn't see him anymore.

While on my watch, I thought about how nice it would've been to be getting off watch (like him) instead of just getting on (like me). I remained there for a little while and then walked to the next location.

At the new location, I stood there watching again, straining my eyes and ears as much as I-- then somebody grabbed me! *I'm going to die!! It's the enemy!!!* But it wasn't the enemy: it was my best friend!

He couldn't contain himself as he laughed and laughed. I kept telling him I could've killed him or something like that, but he kept on laughing. When he calmed down enough to get a few words out, he somehow managed to give me a weak apology. I didn't believe one word of it.

After my best friend left that night, I shook for the next 15 minutes, and it wasn't from the cold or rain. *What if that had been the enemy--it would've been over for me!* That night watch was probably the most afraid I ever was over there because it all happened so fast.

It's funny the things people do at times. I never would have thought that anyone would've stuck around that cold and rainy night just to play a prank on me. And, I have to admit, that I was more alert for the rest of the watch.

We laughed about that night from time to time. Things like that kept us sane so we could get through another day.

HELPING A YOUNG LADY

We got orders that we were going to be the blocking force for the battalion, which meant we'd be helicoptered close to where they thought the enemy soldiers would retreat so they'd run into us when they retreated.

We boarded the helicopters early that morning. After a short flight, we hopped off and moved toward the area we knew the enemy would retreat to. So far, so good.

We were told to keep low and quiet, and move quickly to our designated area. All went well for a while. But then we had to stop short of our destination because the enemy soldiers were already there. As a result, we had to move to our places a lot faster than we wanted to. (We were always prepared for change; we just didn't like that one.)

Given more time, we would've been more prepared for what happened next: they started to come at us through the little river. I can't say all hell broke out, but there was a lot of shooting going on. By the time we got there, they'd already made it to the other side of the river and shot up the place.

One of their bullets went all the way through a young lady's wrist. She'd fallen in the river and was still lying there, holding her injured wrist. Putting my rifle on my shoulder, I reached down and carefully grabbed hold of her arm. *Be careful! Don't use too much pressure.* But somehow my hand accidentally slipped down, and felt the jagged hole left by the bullet. Sliding my arm up closer to her elbow, I held on tighter and managed to get her out of the water. By the time I called for a corpsman to take care of her, the enemy had all but disappeared.

I didn't fire my rifle that day. And I'm sure she was all right because a medevac transported her back to base where she would have received treatment for her injury.

DAYS AND NIGHTS

I'd always thought when the sun went down, the moon came out, but that isn't the way it works at all. I'd never thought much about stuff like that as a civilian--even as a kid--but that all changed my first month over there.

In Vietnam, we counted the days--or should I say nights--when the moon would be out. It seemed like clouds accompanied most of the whole moons, so we could only take advantage of the moonlight by waiting for a space to appear between moving clouds. It was nice to have some light when we were on an ambush or standing guard at night.

Talk about eye strain or hearing strain (if that's even possible)--I couldn't even see my hand in front of my face on most rainy nights. On those nights especially, we focused all of our efforts on seeing and hearing as much as we could.

And while on an ambush, it was even worse since the enemy soldiers could hear us just as easily as we could hear them. We were supposed to be quiet, but sometimes we moved or coughed. And the snores of the person next to you made your heart pound so loud you could hear it.

We didn't care for the heat of the sun, so we liked when it didn't shine so much. With all that said about what it was like when the sun was out, we practically worshipped the moon. But not having the sun meant there would be rain. And if it rained during an operation, they wouldn't send helicopters out or call in support fire.

Are you getting the picture of what it was like to be a Marine in Vietnam? Even the good days weren't good. I could go on and on, and sometimes I do.

FINDING THE ENEMY

Our unit never had much luck finding the enemy. We set up ambush after ambush, humped in the rain and humid heat of day, woke up early and stayed out late--still no enemy.

To remedy this, the powers-that-be came up with a new strategy: we were going to beat the enemy soldiers at their own game by going on patrol at night and sleeping during the day. The whole point of which was to catch them asleep, perhaps even catch them at their base camp.

On the first day of the new strategy, we tried to sleep during the day, but ended up mucking around. We were too concerned about the upcoming night to get any sleep; moreover, we all thought the new strategy was a bad idea.

At dusk, we yawned as we put on our gear and moved out. Everything worked out okay--at first--because there was still some light left. But it wasn't long before we put The Three Stooges to shame.

It must have been a night with no moon because it was dark, dark, and you just can't move a company of Marines through the jungle on a little path, especially at night. Also, the absence of light made it impossible to see anything at all.

We were marching so close to each other that we were stepping on each other's heels, but we stayed like that so we wouldn't get separated from the rest of the column.

Despite our efforts to stay together, half of our column got lost. Some men were sent to find them. When everyone returned, we all got back together and moved out slower than the time before.

We weren't making good time on that so-called patrol. Well-disciplined and well-trained, we just weren't meant for that kind of patrol.

Having so many men moving through the jungle on the darkest of nights just wasn't a good way to sneak up on the enemy. I'm sure the enemy soldiers were laughing at us. They probably figured we were suffering enough already, and that's why they left us alone so we could keep on going.

And keep on going we did, until someone realized he'd left behind his backpack with the map in it. We all had to stop (again) so some men could go back to get it.

Later, we all had to stop to help somebody get back up on the trail after he'd fallen down a hill. It wasn't easygoing. And it had become very dark by that time, too.

We weren't happy. *This patrol's a dumb idea!* The ominous sounds that grew louder as we moved on through the jungle didn't make us feel any better, either.

We did eventually make it to our destination. It was already mid-morning by that time, though.

Despite marching all night, we didn't find the enemy, and the enemy didn't find us. Thank God for that because that wouldn't have been good for us.

That was the first and only time we tried anything like that with a large outfit. We did run other night patrols with squad-size outfits. Those turned out okay (moving around with men you knew really well wasn't that difficult), but maybe they were done in places we knew better.

Believe it or not, but the powers-that-be were the ones who came up with the idea of doing a night patrol with a large outfit. Who knows, maybe it would've worked on a different night, so maybe it was worth a try. But I'm glad we only tried it once.

FLAK JACKETS

During World War II, flak jackets helped protect the Royal Air Force air crews from debris flying through the aircraft and exploding shells. It was a good piece of equipment for stopping metal pieces or even an exploding grenade; it also reduced the seriousness of the injury. But I don't understand why anyone thought it would be a good idea for the infantry person in the bush.

In the jungle, the booby traps were usually on the ground, so their explosions would cause damage to the lower part of the body, not the upper part where the jacket was worn.

If a sniper shot at you, the bullet would have been high enough to go through the jacket and keep right on going. It wouldn't have stopped a rifle's bullet at close range, either.

We also didn't like the unbearable heat that flak jackets trapped inside our chests and backs.

With all that in mind, we figured we didn't need to be carrying around the extra weight of flak jackets.

We soon discovered that we could cut out one or two pieces--about 4 x 4 inches and 1/4 inch thick--from the flak jacket's sides. Nobody said anything about the cut-up flak jackets, and I don't recall anyone ever getting in trouble for having one. (We were careful not to leave any pieces laying around; those were hidden in holes we'd dug at base camp.)

After just a few weeks, our flak jackets had deteriorated to the point where they were basically just nylon jackets with nice pockets that could hold a can of C-Rations and shoulder padding that protected our shoulders from the straps of our backpacks.

Most of us saved the pieces of padding and kept them against our chests. We also used what was left of them as makeshift pillows and blankets.

Even though flak jackets were required on most of our patrols and operations, I don't think removing the padding ever caused anyone harm. Like I explained earlier, they didn't offer much protection from booby traps anyway.

They never issued us replacement flak jackets--the ones we came in with were the same ones we left with. And nobody ever said anything about the ragged condition of the ones we had.

I believe we did the right thing with the flak jackets. We already had too much weight to carry, and they exacerbated our problems with heat, too. Carrying around things that couldn't stop most bullets or protect us from booby traps would've caused more harm than good.

GAS MASKS

The Marine Corps really outdid themselves with the carrying cases for gas masks: they were so good that most of us used them to store personal items--C-Rations, cigarettes, and things like that--everything except the gas masks (those were usually stashed somewhere in our backpacks).

We didn't use, or even think about, our gas masks until we needed them on a large operation several months later. On a short break during that operation, somebody screamed: "GAS!!!" We all scrambled for our gas masks.

Unfortunately, my friend's gas mask must have been at the very bottom of his backpack. As the rest of us frantically searched through our packs, so did he, but he wasn't sure where the hell his was or even if it actually was in there. With tears in his eyes and a runny nose, he eventually gave up and sat back down, determined to suffer through the tear gas without a mask.

Much to the relief of my maskless friend, the wind cleared the air in a minute or two. No worse for the wear, he recovered quickly. Word spread fast and, for the next few months, everyone sought out my friend to hear more about the time he didn't wear a gas mask.

Later that day, we found out that some Marines had thought it would be a good idea to throw tear gas grenades in some nearby caves without warning anyone. (They found nothing in those caves, so that was good.)

I'm not sure if we ever used our gas masks again. They sure had good carrying cases, though. And that was how it sometimes went.

MISCONCEPTIONS

Sometimes, I may sound like I'm not grateful for what people did to make life a little better for us. But what people don't realize is that nothing ever made life easier for that infantryman in the bush; there wasn't a whole lot anyone could do to make life easier out there.

Letters from home and care packages from companies, churches, charities, etc., did help us. Unfortunately, we rarely received the care packages sent to us because they'd be taken by people in the staging area. I don't have proof, but we should've received a lot more care packages than we did.

Regarding USO shows, it's always hard on me when people say how nice it must have been to see all the stars that went to Vietnam for those USO shows. What they didn't--and still don't--understand was that we didn't get to see the shows unless we were entering or leaving Vietnam. There again, it was mostly personnel in the back area who would get to see the shows. The only shows we saw were those playing out in front of us on patrols and ambushes. And what we were really looking for was water we could drink and people who were trying to kill us.

You hear a lot about the drugs that were over there, but marijuana was the only one I was aware of. People would bring it back when they returned from R&R, then the air would smell like grass that night and maybe the next, but that was about it.

Many people think that 50 or so of us rode everywhere in helicopters, but that wasn't how things worked in the Marine Corps. Most of our patrols were small--maybe nine or ten men. Also, our main form of transportation was humping, not helicopters.

AMTRACS SHOULDN'T BE ABLE TO FLOAT

I'm not sure if you know that the AmTrac is like--or could be compared to--the bumblebee: the bumblebee shouldn't be able to fly, and the AmTrac shouldn't be able to float. The last time I rode in an AmTrac, that bumblebee comparison wouldn't leave my mind

On that day, we were going in as a blocking force, which meant that other Marines would be chasing the enemy soldiers toward us. The enemy soldiers didn't know where we were or where we were going, but somehow they always knew because they just knew things like that.

We boarded an AmTrac for our trip across a large river. Even though it was a little hot inside, it sure beat walking.

I didn't like riding on AmTracs because I knew that a motor failure would cause an AmTrac to slowly sink due to the sump pumps losing power. If that happened, there wouldn't be much time to get the stopped engine running again.

The AmTrac we were in wasn't going very fast in the water and was only staying a few inches out of it. The motor stopped when we were most of the way across the river. They tried and tried to get it running again with no luck. We couldn't make out what the crew men were saying in raised voices, but we knew it wasn't good.

There was a lot of fear in that little iron box that day: we all knew it was going to sink. Men started taking off their gear, helmets, flak jackets, and packs so they'd be ready to make a swim for it.

There were no life jackets on that AmTrac. I don't know if there were supposed to be or not, but I know there weren't any because if there were, I wouldn't have been so afraid.

I knew I couldn't swim that well and that I would drown and there was no doubt about it. *If this AmTrac goes down, I'm going down with it!* With that in mind, I didn't even bother taking off my boots or any of my gear.

It's hard to imagine the fear a person feels knowing the end is near. I'm sure I made my peace with my maker, and that was about it.

Then the engine finally caught--*Thank you, God*--and we started moving again. You could feel the relief of everyone aboard. In my heart, I knew I was saved... for that day.

THE DAY WE TOOK BACK KHE SANH

I'm sure that most people reading this know all about Khe Sanh and how the Marines held it for so long. They were surrounded and had artillery on them day and night.

Their daily supplies had to come from airplanes because there was no way to get anything to them by land. The enemy soldiers had all the roads blocked with a superior force to stop anyone from making it through to the outpost.

With everything that was going on around them, it was a daily struggle for the Marines just to stay alive and keep their wits about them. Despite the airplane strikes over and around the area to keep the enemy soldiers back, they continued to push on and on.

We couldn't knock out the enemy's artillery because they were hidden in the mountains. I'm sure we got some of them, but there were always more, so the shelling on Khe Sanh continued day after day.

Despite being always on alert, running patrols to keep any large forces from getting too close, and overtaking part of the perimeter, the Marines lost quite a few men there. It was quite pricey all the way around, but we didn't want to let it go. We didn't want to be like the French had been quite a few years earlier when they surrendered after the enemy finally got to them. Instead, we were making a statement that we would stand the line no matter what.

The enemy eventually backed off, probably because that outpost wasn't really that important. They tore it down and moved on to another part of the country. There wasn't much said about taking Khe Sanh back after that.

Later, the powers-that-be wanted to make everything official by having us declare that we were taking Khe Sanh back, even though we'd never lost it or given it up. I guess they wanted some headlines about how the Marines went back to Khe Sanh and showed the enemy who was boss.

When we arrived in Khe Sanh to take it back, we received a grand reception: flags were everywhere, a band was playing, and speakers were announcing over the PA system how great and proud we were to be taking back Khe Sanh.

Then everything ended and we were dismissed. The members of the band and the speakers were returned to the back area on helicopters. We rode back on trucks.

The good part was that we didn't lose anyone or even receive any incoming fire when we took back Khe Sanh. All I remember is we arrived, there was a big production, then everything ended. Sometimes, you just have to laugh at what really goes on behind the scenes.

COLD DRINKS

For a short time, our base camp was near a village where we could purchase sodas and ice. We weren't there very long--we were always on the move--but it was nice while it lasted.

We decided to make the most of that location by creating a meeting spot where we could relax and pretend we were in a park, or something like that. Draping some camouflage netting over a few trees, we arranged some empty ammo boxes under it so we'd have a place to sit and talk and enjoy cold drinks.

When we heard that we'd be going on a large operation soon, we thought it would be nice to come back to some ice-cold beverages for a change; all we needed was some way to keep the drinks cold.

We made a refrigerator of sorts with an ammo box, an old poncho, and some ice. But we weren't done yet: since sawdust was used in the old days to keep ice from melting so fast, we decided to use rice hulls the same way. We then moved the ammo box with that precious cargo inside to a shady spot and covered it with a sandbag.

On the large operation the next day, our thoughts kept drifting back to how great it was going to be to drink ice-cold sodas when we returned to camp. We grinned at each other and thought about how smart we were to have come up with that idea.

When we got back to camp a week later--most big operations lasted a week or so--we couldn't wait to get to our ammo box with the cold drinks inside. But what we discovered was that our ammo box wasn't cold at all. In fact, it was quite warm! The rice hulls that were supposed to prevent the ice from melting so fast hadn't done their job at all. We would've been better off just putting the sodas in the shade. But we at least got to enjoy our new meeting place while we drank the warm sodas and laughed.

Little things like that kept us going. As long as we had people we could trust and a little time to ourselves, we would make it.

Made in United States
Orlando, FL
10 May 2022

17736805R00050